How to
Reach Your Favorite
Sports Star III

▼▼▼▼▼

How to Reach Your Favorite Sports Star III

▼▼▼▼▼

Dylan B. Tomlinson

Lowell House Juvenile
Los Angeles
• • • • •
Contemporary Books
Chicago

For Fred, who always found an extra ticket for his nephew

Publisher: Jack Artenstein
Associate Publisher, Juvenile Division: Elizabeth Amos
Director of Publishing Services: Rena Copperman
Managing Editor, Juvenile Division: Lindsey Hay
Editor in Chief, Nonfiction Juvenile: Amy Downing
Editorial Assistant: Inga Herrmann

Library of Congress Catalog Card Number is available.

ISBN: 1-56565-709-8

Lowell House books can be purchased at special discounts
when ordered in bulk for premiums and special sales.
Contact Department JH at the following address:

Lowell House Juvenile
2029 Century Park East, Suite 3290
Los Angeles, CA 90067

Manufactured in the United States of America

10 9 8 7 6 5 4 3 2

Contents

▼▼▼▼▼▼▼▼▼▼▼▼▼▼▼▼▼▼▼

Reach out and touch your favorite sports star!

*I*f you've ever had the impulse to tell a special sports celeb exactly how you feel, grab a pen and do it now! But how do you reach your favorite sports stars? It's easy. Read about them in the following pages, then write to the address that accompanies each entry. For best results, remember the following:

➤ Don't obsess about spelling, grammar, and/or sounding foolish. These are fan letters you're writing, not English compositions. Remember to have fun!

➤ If you want a reply, it's best to send a self-addressed, stamped envelope (SASE) along with your letter. That's an envelope with a first-class postage stamp and your name and address printed legibly on it.

➤ If you are writing to or from a country other than the United States (for instance, if you are in Canada writing to a star at a U.S. address), you will need to include international postage coupons with your letter. You can purchase international postage coupons at any post office.

➤ Sports stars change addresses and teams just like anybody else. But even if the person you write to is long gone, your letter should be forwarded to his or her new address.

Andre Agassi

Tennis Player

□ □ □ □ □ □ □ □ □ □ □ □ □ □ □ □ □ □

*N*o player in the history of tennis has ever done more to promote the sport than Agassi. In the late 1980s tennis was rapidly losing popularity with young people. That ended immediately when Agassi went pro in 1987 at the age of sixteen. Known for his bandanas, his denim shorts, and playing "rock'n'roll" tennis, Agassi began filling stands with young fans before he had even gotten his driver's license at age seventeen. Almost ten years later, he is still the most popular athlete in the game. Agassi can never be accused of having more flash than substance, though, since he is one of the leading players in the world.

So You Want to Know—

If rivalries can be friendly? Andre and Pete Sampras make up possibly the fiercest rivalry in tennis history. The two have flip-flopped the number one and two positions for over two years. The two superstars remain tied in head-to-head battles. Off the court, Sampras and Agassi are close friends. Both were on the U.S. Davis Cup team, and they appear together in a Nike ad.

Birthday Beat
April 29, 1970

Cool Credits
➤ Winner of 31 career titles
➤ Won ATP Championship, 1990
➤ Won Wimbledon, 1992
➤ Won U.S. Open, 1993, 1994
➤ Won Australian Open, 1995
➤ Ranked No. 1 in the world, April 10, 1995
➤ Led U.S. to Davis Cup Championships, 1992–95

Vital Stats
➤ Height: 5'11"
➤ Weight: 165
➤ Birthplace: Las Vegas, Nevada
➤ Current residence: Las Vegas, Nevada
➤ Engaged to: Brooke Shields

The Andre Agassi Fan Club
One Bowerman Dr.
Beaverton, OR 97005
or
Andre Agassi
Agassi Enterprises
2300 Sahara Ave., #1150
Las Vegas, NV 89102

Troy Aikman
Quarterback, Dallas Cowboys

▼▼▼▼▼▼▼▼▼

Cool Credits

➤ NCAA all-American at UCLA, 1988
➤ First pick in the 1989 draft by the Cowboys
➤ Led Cowboys to Super Bowl victories, 1993, 1994, 1996
➤ Super Bowl MVP, 1993
➤ All-pro five consecutive seasons, 1991–95

Vital Stats

➤ Height: 6'4"
➤ Weight: 228
➤ Birthplace: West Covina, California
➤ Current residence: Irving, Texas
➤ Favorite foods: pizza and spaghetti
➤ Nickname: T-Roy
➤ T.V. debut: Troy once played himself on an episode of the TV show "Coach."

Birthday Beat

November 21, 1966

So You Want to Know—

How many times Barry Switzer has coached Aikman? After playing one season at the University of Oklahoma, Aikman went to OU head coach Barry Switzer and asked him if he would okay a transfer to another school that passes the ball more often. Switzer obliged, giving the green light for Aikman to transfer to UCLA in 1986. Nine years later, Aikman and Switzer met again when Switzer was hired as the head coach of the Dallas Cowboys.

After winning his third Super Bowl title in 1996, Aikman solidified his place in history as one of the best quarterbacks to ever play in the NFL. Only Terry Bradshaw and Joe Montana have led their teams to more Super Bowl titles than Aikman has. Aikman has also been with the Cowboys through the bad times. After joining Dallas as a rookie in 1989, Aikman was forced to sit back and watch as the Cowboys finished 1–15, the worst record in franchise history. Another man would have been afraid of what was ahead for the Cowboys, but not Aikman, who just two seasons later led Dallas to a Super Bowl victory. Aikman is one of the true great quarterbacks in the NFL.

Troy Aikman Fan Club
P.O. Box 201326
Arlington, TX 76011
or
Troy Aikman
c/o The Dallas Cowboys
One Cowboys Parkway
Irving, TX 75063

Dante Bichette

Rightfielder, Colorado Rockies

■ ■ ■ ■ ■ ■ ■ ■ ■ ■ ■ ■ ■ ■ ■ ■

*C*an you say instant impact? In 1993, the Rockies were a struggling expansion team that finished with one of the worst records in the National League. Two years later, they made the playoffs, and much of the credit belongs to Dante. Bichette amazed everyone when he lead the National League in home runs and runs batted in (RBIs). For his efforts, Bichette was the runner-up for league MVP and was named to the all-star team.

So You Want to Know—

What Dante's good luck charm is? Dante refused to cut his hair during the 1995 season because he thought it brought him good luck. Maybe he was onto something—he was one of the most productive hitters in the majors that season. Apparently, Coach Don Baylor didn't buy the good luck charm theory. He made Dante get a haircut before beginning the 1996 season.

Birthday Beat
November 18, 1963

Cool Credits
➤ National League all-star, 1994, 1995
➤ Runner-up for National League MVP, 1995
➤ The *Sporting News* Player of the Year, 1995

Vital Stats
➤ Height: 6'3"
➤ Weight: 212
➤ Birthplace: West Palm Beach, Florida
➤ Current residence: Long Beach, California
➤ Favorite food: Mexican
➤ Nickname: Inferno

Dante Bichette
c/o The Colorado Rockies
1700 Broadway, Suite 2100
Denver, CO 80290

Craig Biggio

Second Baseman, Houston Astros

□ □ □ □ □ □ □ □ □ □ □ □ □ □ □ □ □ □ □

Biggio has been a quiet superstar for the past decade, at two different positions. Biggio was originally drafted as a catcher, but when the Astros needed a second baseman, Biggio was more than happy to change positions for the good of his team. In the beginning of Biggio's career he was often overshadowed by his teammate, first baseman Jeff Bagwell. Now, Craig is casting a shadow of his own as one of the top hitting and fielding second basemen in the majors.

So You Want to Know—
If baseball positions are interchangable? While several players have been all-stars at more than one related position (like second baseman and third baseman), Biggio is the only player in major league history to make the all-star team at the unrelated positions of catcher and second baseman.

Vital Stats
➤ Height: 5'11"
➤ Weight: 180
➤ Birthplace: Smithtown, New York
➤ Current residence: Spring Lake, New Jersey
➤ Favorite food: hamburgers

Cool Credits

➤ All-American at Seton Hall, 1987
➤ First round draft choice by the Astros, 1987
➤ Silver Slugger Winner, the player at his position to hit the most home runs, 1989, 1994, 1995
➤ All-star, 1989, 1991, 1992, 1994, 1995
➤ Led National League with 123 runs scored, 1995
➤ Golden Glove winner, most catches of any second baseman, 1994, 1995

Birthday Beat
December 14, 1965

• •

Craig Biggio
c/o The Houston Astros
The Astrodome
P.O. Box 288
Houston, Texas 77001-0288

• •

Jeff Blake

Quarterback, Cincinnati Bengals

▼▼▼▼▼▼▼▼▼▼▼▼▼▼▼▼▼▼▼

*A*fter sitting on the bench for two years as a New York Jet, Blake signed with the Bengals in 1994 as the backup quarterback to David Klingler. Blake didn't stay on the bench for too long. He became the starter after Klingler was hurt early in the 1994 season, and was so impressive that he remained as starter even after Klingler's return. Blake's outstanding play continued into the 1995 season, in which he and wide receiver Carl Pickens became the most feared duo in the AFC.

Birthday Beat
December 4, 1970

16

Vital Stats

➤ Height: 6'
➤ Weight: 200
➤ Birthplace: Sanford, Florida
➤ Current residence: Cincinnati, Ohio
➤ Hobby: playing baseball
➤ Favorite food: chicken

Cool Credits

➤ 2nd Team all-American at East Carolina, 1991
➤ Led East Carolina to their highest national ranking (#10) in school history, 1991
➤ AFC Player of the Month, November 1994
➤ Led the AFC in touchdown passes, 1995
➤ NFL Pro Bowl, 1995

So You Want to Know—

If Blake cares about kids' reading habits? In 1995 Blake sponsored a Cincinnati school district program that gave school kids an incentive to read. In exchange for reading a required number of books, Blake gave the kids free Bengals tickets.

Jeff Blake
c/o The Cincinnati Bengals
Riverfront Stadium
100 Pete Rose Way
Cincinnati, OH 45202

Drew Bledsoe

Quarterback, New England Patriots

■ ■ ■ ■ ■ ■ ■ ■ ■ ■ ■ ■ ■ ■ ■

Vital Stats

➤ Height: 6'5"
➤ Weight: 233
➤ Birthplace:
Ellensburg, Washington
➤ Current residence:
Ellensburg, Washington
➤ Hobby: hunting
➤ College: Washington
State University
➤ Majored in: education
at WSU

Cool Credits

➤ 2nd team all-American,
1992
➤ All-Pac 10, 1992
➤ First pick in the 1993
draft
➤ All-rookie team, 1993
➤ All-pro, 1994

Birthday Beat

*February 14,
1972*

Drew has given new meaning to the term "Young Gun" in his three seasons in the NFL. After being the first pick in the 1993 NFL Draft, Bledsoe went to New England on a mission to prove his worth to the Patriots. He has done just that by leading the team in passing for each of his three seasons. Just twenty-four years old, Bledsoe should be giving Patriot fans a lot to cheer about for years to come.

> **So You Want to Know—**
> If Bledsoe has strong family ties? He loves his grandfather Stu so much that after signing with the Patriots, he established the $150,000 Stu Bledsoe scholarship fund at Washington State.

Drew Bledsoe
c/o New England Patriots
Foxboro Route 1
Foxboro, MA 02035

Chris Chelios

Defenseman, Chicago Blackhawks

□ □ □ □ □ □ □ □ □ □ □ □ □ □ □ □ □ □ □

*W*hile many hockey players, like Wayne Gretzky and Mark Messier, are known for scoring goals, Chelios is known for being an enforcer. As one of the roughest players in the NHL, the powerful Chelios forces other players to look over their shoulders for fear of being knocked down. While best known for his aggressive play, Chelios is also considered the best defenseman in the league. A nine time all-star and a former Olympian, Chelios

is a major reason the Blackhawks are one of the best teams in the NHL.

Cool Credits
➤ Had four assists in the 1984 Olympics at Sarajevo
➤ Won the James Norris Memorial Trophy, 1993
➤ First team all-NHL, 1993, 1995, 1996

Birthday Beat
January 25, 1962

Vital Stats
➤ Height: 6'1"
➤ Weight: 190
➤ Birthplace: Chicago, Illinois
➤ Current residence: Chicago, Illinois
➤ Favorite food: Polish sausage

• •

Chris Chelios
c/o The Chicago Blackhawks
The United Center
Chicago, IL 60611

21

• •

Laura Davies

Golfer

▼▼▼▼▼▼▼▼▼▼▼▼▼▼▼▼▼▼

*F*ew women have had the kind of impact on their sport that Laura Davies has had on golf. Davies joined the LPGA Tour in 1987, and as tour rookie, won the U.S. Women's Open, one of the biggest events on the tour. Idolized in her native England, as well as around the world, Davies continues to be the dominant force in the LPGA. She wins more events than any other woman on the tour and shows no sign of letting up.

Birthday Beat
October 5, 1963

Vital Stats

➤ Height: 5'10"
➤ Weight: 170
➤ Birthplace: Coventry, England
➤ Current residence: West Byfleet, England

So You Want to Know—

Where England's top golfer likes to dine? It's not at any fancy restaurants with England's other top athletes. Davies admits her favorite restaurant is Wimpy's, named after the Popeye character. It's England's equivalent of McDonalds, and she rarely eats out anywhere else!

➤ Hobbies: races greyhounds, collects television sets
➤ Favorite pastime: pool
➤ Favorite food: hamburgers
➤ Favorite author: William Shakespeare
➤ Personal parade: After Laura won the 1987 U.S. Women's Open, the Brits threw a parade in her honor, and over 1000 fans met her plane when she landed in England.

Cool Credits

➤ Named a Member of the British Empire, one of Britain's highest honors, 1988
➤ LPGA Championship winner, 1994
➤ Sara Lee Classic Winner, 1994

Laura Davies
c/o LPGA Headquarters
2750 W. International Speedway Blvd., Suite B
Daytona Beach, FL 32114

Marshall Faulk

Running Back, Indianapolis Colts

So You Want to Know—

How badly Marshall wanted to play running back? Coming out of high school, Marshall was only being recruited by colleges as a defensive back. San Diego State was the only school who told him he could play running back, and he rewarded them with three consecutive all-American seasons during his freshman, sophomore, and junior seasons before going pro.

Cool Credits

➤ 2nd Team all-American at East Carolina, 1991
➤ Led East Carolina to their highest national ranking (#10) in school history, 1991
➤ AFC Player of the Month, November 1994
➤ Led the AFC in touchdown passes, 1995
➤ NFL Pro Bowl, 1995

Vital Stats

➤ Height: 5'10"
➤ Weight: 205
➤ Birthplace: New Orleans, Louisiana

➤ Current residence: New Orleans, Louisiana
➤ Hobbies: playing basketball
➤ Favorite food: jambalaya
➤ College attended: San Diego State
➤ Scoop on the Marshall Plan: donates $2,000 per touchdown he scores to The Marshall Plan, which helps inner-city youth in Indianapolis, New Orleans, and San Diego.
➤ Post-touchdown activity: After every touchdown, Marshall sends the football to his mother in New Orleans.

*W*hen talking about the best young players in the NFL, one cannot help but mention Marshall Faulk. In just two seasons, Marshall has already made a name for himself. Faulk rushed for over 1,000 yards each season, a feat duplicated by only eight other players. For his efforts, Faulk was selected by the media, coaches, and other players to play in the Pro Bowl after both the 1994 and 1995 seasons.

Birthday Beat
February 26, 1973

Marshall Faulk
c/o The Indianapolis Colts
Indianapolis, IN 46204

Peter Forsberg

Center, Colorado Avalanche

🔲 🔲 🔲 🔲 🔲 🔲 🔲 🔲 🔲 🔲 🔲 🔲 🔲 🔲 🔲 🔲 🔲

*A*fter only two seasons in the NHL, Forsberg has already become one of the best centers in the league. As a rookie with the Quebec Nordiques, Forsberg was so impressive that he was named Rookie of the Year. In his second season, with the Colorado Avalanche, he was named to the all-star team. Forsberg hasn't only impressed hockey fans on this continent. He became a national hero in his native country of Sweden after scoring the winning goal in the 1994 Winter Olympics.

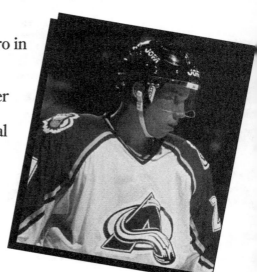

Birthday Beat
July 20, 1973

Vital Stats

➤ Height: 5'11"
➤ Weight: 190
➤ Birthplace: Ornskoldvik, Sweden
➤ Current residence: Denver during hockey season; Sweden the rest of the year
➤ Nickname: The nickname of the Avalanche front line of Forsberg, Joe Sakic, and Valeri Kamensky is the Barrage a Trois.
➤ Hobby: fishing

Cool Credits

➤ NHL Rookie of the Year, 1995
➤ All-star, 1996

So You Want to Know—

How well-known Peter is? Forsberg is so famous in Sweden that his likeness appears on a postage stamp. He is the only hockey player to have been given such an honor.

Peter Forsberg
c/o The Colorado Avalanche
McNichols Sports Complex
1635 Clay St.
Denver, CO 80204

Steffi Graf

Tennis Player

▼▼▼▼▼▼▼▼▼▼▼▼▼▼▼▼▼▼▼

Vital Stats

➤ Height: 5'9"
➤ Weight: 135
➤ Birthplace: Mannheim, Germany
➤ Current residence: Del Rey Beach, Florida
➤ Hobbies: reading horror novels
➤ Favorite food: Italian
➤ Photo moments: has modeled for *Vogue* magazine

Cool Credits

➤ Turned pro, 1984
➤ Olympic gold medal, 1988
➤ Olympic silver medal, 1992
➤ No. 1 ranked player in the world, 1987–1990, 1993–1996
➤ Winner of twenty Grand Slam events

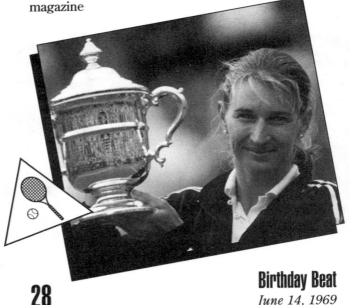

Birthday Beat
June 14, 1969

*N*o player has ever dominated women's tennis the way Steffi Graf has. Graf quietly worked her way to the top of the women's pro tour when all of the attention was on Chris Evert and Martina Navratilova. But in 1989, all of the focus shifted to Graf, who became the first player in over twenty years to win all four Grand Slam events in the same year. In fact, Graf finished the year with an unbelievable 136–2 record! Graf currently remains the world's top ranked women's tennis player and shows no signs of letting up.

So You Want to Know—

Who German girls want to be like when they grow up? Well, Steffi of course! In a 1995 poll of schoolgirls aged six to fourteen, Steffi was the overwhelming choice when asked which woman they most admired.

Steffi Graf
c/o *Advantage International, Inc.*
1751 Pinnacle Dr., Suite 1500
McLean, VA 22102

Ken Griffey, Jr.

Outfielder, Seattle Mariners

■ ■ ■ ■ ■ ■ ■ ■ ■ ■ ■ ■ ■ ■ ■ ■

*T*here are very few sure things in professional sports, but when Ken Griffey, Jr. entered the baseball draft in 1987, baseball got a sure thing. In eight years in the majors, Griffey has been an all-star six times, and is always among the league leaders in home runs, RBIs, and batting average. He is also one of the best fielders in baseball. Known for his tendency to leap over the outfield fences to catch balls, Griffey has won three Golden Glove Awards for being the best left fielder in the majors. Whether it's at the plate or in the field, Griffey is a force to be reckoned with.

Cool Credits

➤ United States High School Player of the Year, 1987
➤ First round draft pick by the Seattle Mariners, 1987
➤ American League all-star, 1990–1995
➤ All-star MVP, 1992
➤ Led the Mariners to their first Division Title, 1995

Vital Stats

➤ Height: 6'3"
➤ Weight: 205
➤ Birthplace: Donora, Pennsylvania
➤ Current residence: Seattle, Washington
➤ Favorite food: chicken

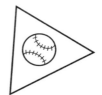

30

Birthday Beat
November 21, 1969

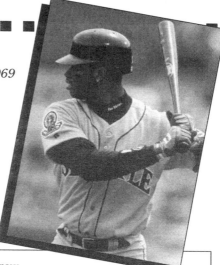

So You Want to Know—
If talent runs in the family? Ken Griffey and Ken Griffey, Jr. were briefly teammates on the Mariners, and on September 17, 1990, they hit back-to-back home runs. It remains to be seen if Griffey, Jr.'s son Trey Kenneth Griffey III will ever have the opportunity to play with his father, but with the talent in the Griffey family, most people wouldn't doubt it.

Ken Griffey, Jr.
c/o The Seattle Mariners
The Kingdome
201 S. King St.
Seattle, WA 98104

Mia Hamm

Forward, U.S. National Soccer Team

*A*nybody who thinks that only men can play soccer has obviously never seen Mia Hamm in action. Mia is to women's soccer what Michael Jordan is to the NBA. She is widely considered to be the best female soccer player in the world, has scored more goals than any other U.S. woman soccer player, and has even outplayed the best players on the University of North Carolina men's team. Mia led the University of North Carolina to four national titles while she was in college, and is now looking to lead the U.S. Women's team to the World Championships.

So You Want to Know—

What a great player Mia is? While many players work their entire lives to be able to play on the U.S. National Team, Mia played on it when she was a fifteen-year-old high school sophomore—the youngest member of the team ever.

☐ ☐ ☐ ☐ ☐ ☐ ☐ ☐ ☐ ☐ ☐ ☐ ☐ ☐ ☐ ☐ ☐ ☐ ☐

Cool Credits

➤ All-American at the University of North Carolina, 1990, 1992, 1993
➤ Led the University of North Carolina to NCAA Titles, 1990–1993
➤ Led the team in scoring and assists, 1995
➤ MVP of the Women's Cup, 1994
➤ Female Soccer Athlete of the Year, 1994, 1995

Birthday Beat

May 17, 1972

Vital Stats

➤ Height: 5'5"
➤ Weight: 125
➤ Birthplace: Selma, Alabama
➤ Current residence: Chapel Hill, North Carolina

Mia Hamm
c/o U.S. Soccer Federation
1801-11 South Prairie Ave.
Chicago, IL 60616

Anfernee Hardaway

Guard, Orlando Magic

▼▼▼▼▼▼▼▼▼▼▼▼▼▼▼▼▼

Rarely has there been a duo as young and as talented as the Orlando Magic's Shaquille O'Neal and Anfernee Hardaway. The Magic became a good team when they acquired Shaq, but once they added Hardaway, they became one of the best teams in the league. Coaches love Hardaway for his leadership abilities and his desire to win on and off the court. He is a player who refuses to lose and who demands the best from his teammates.

Cool Credits

➤ All-American at University of Memphis, 1993
➤ Runner-up for Rookie of the Year, 1994
➤ NBA all-star, 1995, 1996
➤ Member of the 1996 Olympic Team

So You Want to Know—

How Anfernee got the nickname Penny? When Hardaway was just twelve years old, one of his youth league coaches kept saying, "If I had a penny for every time that kid made a great play, I'd be a rich man." The nickname stuck.

34

Birthday Beat
July 18, 1972

Vital Stats

➤ Height: 6'7"
➤ Weight: 210
➤ Birthplace: Memphis, Tennessee
➤ Current residence: Orlando, Florida
➤ Nickname: Penny

➤ Favorite food: hamburgers
➤ Commericials: Hardaway and comedian Chris Rock star together in some of Nike's most famous ads.

Anfernee Hardaway
c/o Orlando Magic
Orlando Arena
One Magic Place
Orlando, FL 32801

Grant Hill

Forward, Detroit Pistons

■ ■ ■ ■ ■ ■ ■ ■ ■ ■ ■

Cool Credits

➤ Won National Championships at Duke, 1991, 1992
➤ Selected by Pistons with the third pick in the 1994 NBA Draft
➤ Co-Rookie of the Year, 1995
➤ NBA All-star, 1995, 1996

Vital Stats

➤ Height: 6'8"
➤ Weight: 225
➤ Birthplace: Dallas, Texas
➤ Current residence: Detroit, Michigan
➤ Family Ties: Grant is the son of former Dallas Cowboy running back Calvin Hill.
➤ College: Duke University, 1994
➤ Majored in: economics

Birthday Beat

October 5, 1972

■ ■ ■ ■ ■ ■ ■ ■ ■ ■ ■ ■ ■ ■ ■ ■ ■ ■

*S*uccess follows Grant Hill wherever he goes. He won two National Championships at Duke University, and has kept the Pistons at the top of the NBA ladder with his tremendous shooting, rebounding, and ferocious dunking. In just two years in the NBA, Hill has already become one of its most popular players. In 1995 and 1996, he received more votes from fans to start in the all-star game than any other player in the league.

So You Want to Know—

If athletes can be role models? While Grant Hill loves playing in the NBA, he gets more satisfaction participating in various Detroit area charities. Hill considers it an honor that any kid would see him as a role model.

Grant Hill
c/o Detroit Pistons
2 Championship Dr.
Auburn Hills, MI 48362

Juwan Howard

Forward, Washington Bullets

□ □ □ □ □ □ □ □ □ □ □ □ □ □ □ □ □ □ □

Cool Credits

➤ High School Player of the Year, 1991
➤ Played in NCAA title game, 1992, 1993

Vital Stats

➤ Height: 6'9"
➤ Weight: 250
➤ Birthplace: Chicago, Illinois
➤ Current residence: Washington D.C.
➤ College: University of Michigan at Ann Arbor, 1995
➤ Majored in: economics

Birthday Beat
February 7, 1973

□ □ □ □ □ □ □ □ □ □ □ □ □ □ □ □

*A*s a member of the Fab Five at the University of Michigan from 1991–1993, Howard was constantly overshadowed by teammates Chris Webber (Washington Bullets) and Jalen Rose (Denver Nuggets). He stepped out of the shadows in the NBA. As a rookie in 1995, Howard was named to the second squad for the all-rookie team. In 1996, Howard was selected as a member of the NBA all-star team. At just twenty-three years old, Juwan Howard has already established himself as one of the best young players in the NBA.

So You Want to Know—

If Howard cares about education? Upon leaving the University of Michigan at Ann Arbor after his junior season to enter the NBA, Howard promised his mother he would go back to school and earn his degree. He kept his promise to his mother by earning his degree in May of 1995, and graduating with his class in just four years.

Juwan Howard
c/o Washington Bullets
One North Harry S. Truman Dr.
Landover, MD 20785

Chipper Jones
Third Baseman, Atlanta Braves

▼▼▼▼▼▼▼▼▼▼▼▼▼▼▼▼▼▼▼

*J*ones had the kind of rookie season in 1995 that most players can only dream about. After playing well during the regular season, he performed like a seasoned pro throughout the playoffs. With feats like a game-winning home run to clinch the first round against Colorado, Jones proved to be a major factor in bringing Atlanta their first championship ever.

Cool Credits

➤ United States High School Player of the Year, 1990
➤ First pick in the 1990 baseball draft by the Braves
➤ Runner-up for National League Rookie of the Year, 1995
➤ The *Sporting News* Rookie of the Year, 1995

Vital Stats

➤ Height: 6'3"
➤ Weight: 200
➤ Birthplace: DeLand, Florida
➤ Current residence: Marietta, Georgia
➤ Nickname: Chip Shot
➤ Hobbies: hunting and fishing
➤ Favorite food: pizza

Birthday Beat

April 24, 1972

So You Want to Know—

What's old-fashioned about Chipper? He is one of the only baseball players to wear his pants tucked inside his stirrups like the old timer players used to do.

Chipper Jones
c/o The Atlanta Braves
P.O. Box 4064
Atlanta, GA 30302

Cobi Jones

Midfielder, Los Angeles Galaxy

■ ■ ■ ■ ■ ■ ■ ■ ■ ■ ■ ■ ■ ■ ■ ■ ■

Whether he was playing for UCLA, the U.S. World Cup Team, or the Major League Soccer Federation, Cobi has dominated at every level. Jones is known for his flashy speed and his trademark shoulder-length dread locks. A big contributor in the World Cup, Jones helped lead the United States to their best finish in over fifty years. Jones impressed so many people across the world that he was one of only a handful of Americans asked to play in the European leagues. Though that is the highest compliment that can be paid an American soccer player, Jones decided to play for the Galaxy in 1996 to be close to his hometown. He is a major reason why soccer is becoming more and more popular in the United States today.

Birthday Beat
June 16, 1970

■ ■ ■ ■ ■ ■ ■ ■ ■ ■ ■ ■ ■ ■ ■ ■ ■

Cool Credits

➤ All-American at UCLA, 1991
➤ Member of the United States Olympic Team, 1992
➤ Played for Coventry City in the British Soccer League, 1994–1996
➤ Fastest player on the U.S. World Cup team
➤ Played in every game for the United States in 1994's World Cup

Vital Stats

➤ Height: 5'7"
➤ Weight: 145
➤ Birthplace: Westlake Village, California
➤ Current residence: Los Angeles, California
➤ Favorite food: Mexican

➤ Star connections: One of Cobi's teammates on the Galaxy is *Melrose Place* star Andrew Shue

So You Want to Know—

What Cobi thinks about the rise in popularity of soccer in the U.S.? Cobi believes that since soccer is the most popular sport in the world, it was inevitable that the sport would eventually catch on in the U.S. With America's strong showing in the 1994 World Cup and the development of major league soccer in the states, Cobi says that soccer is here to stay.

Cobi Jones
c/o U.S. Soccer Federation
1801-11 South Prairie Ave.
Chicago, IL 60616

Michael Jordan

Shooting Guard, Chicago Bulls

□ □ □ □ □ □ □ □ □ □ □ □ □ □ □ □ □ □

Perhaps the greatest basketball player who has ever lived, Jordan has led the Bulls to three back-to-back NBA titles. A five-time MVP, Jordan also led the University of North Carolina to the NCAA title in 1982, and the Bulls to the best record in NBA history when they went 72–10 in the 1995–96 season. It would be tough to argue that any player has had as much impact on basketball as Michael Jordan has had.

Cool Credits

➤ Won Olympic gold medal, 1984, 1992
➤ Led the Bulls to NBA title, 1991–1993
➤ Won the NBA MVP, 1988, 1990, 1991, 1993, 1996

➤ NBA all-star, 1985, 1987–1993, 1996
➤ NBA scoring leader, 1987–1993, 1996

Birthday Beat

February 17, 1963

44

Vital Stats

➤ Height: 6'6"
➤ Weight: 200
➤ Birthplace: Brooklyn, New York
➤ Current residence: Northbrook, Illinois
➤ Nickname: Air
➤ Favorite food: hamburgers
➤ Hobby: golf
➤ New shoes: Jordan wears a new pair of shoes for every game. When he's done with them, he autographs them, auctions them off, then donates the money to Chicago area charities.

➤ Old shorts: Jordan wears his college basketball shorts under his Bulls uniform shorts for every game that he plays.
➤ College: University of North Carolina at Chapel Hill

So You Want to Know—

How Michael spends his free time? Jordan spends much of his free time with his family, but he also likes to hang out at his own Chicago hamburger restaurant, called Michael's.

Michael Jordan
Air Jordan Flight Club
c/o Ryan Morland
One Bowerman Dr.
Beaverton, OR 97005
or
Michael Jordan
c/o Chicago Bulls
1 Magnificent Mile
980 N. Michigan Ave.#11600
Chicago, IL 60611-4501

Paul Kariya

Forward, Anaheim Mighty Ducks

▼▼▼▼▼▼▼▼▼▼▼▼▼▼▼▼▼▼▼▼

Vital Stats

➤ Height: 5'11"
➤ Weight: 175
➤ Birthplace: Vancouver, British Columbia
➤ Current residence: Vancouver, British Columbia

Cool Credits

➤ Led the University of Maine to the NCAA Title, 1993
➤ All-American, 1993
➤ Led Team Canada to the silver medal in the Winter Olympics, 1994
➤ Led all rookies in scoring, 1995
➤ NHL all-star, 1996

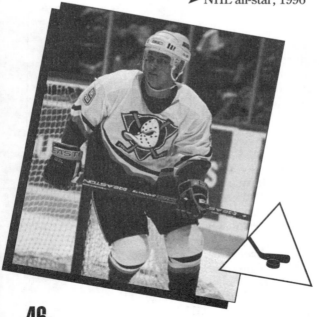

F ew players enjoy the kind of impact in terms of scoring and popularity that Kariya has had in just two seasons in the NHL.

After being edged out in 1995 by Colorado's Peter Forsberg as the NHL Rookie of the Year, Kariya came back with a vengeance. He scored 108 points in his sophomore season, and if Anaheim fans are lucky, they'll see plenty more from this talented young superstar.

> **So You Want to Know—**
> What Paul does in his spare time? When he's not on the ice, Paul likes to spend his free time in various Los Angeles dance clubs . . . on the dance floor!

Birthday Beat
October 16, 1974

Paul Kariya
c/o Arrowhead Pond of Anaheim
2695 East Katella Ave.
Anaheim, CA 92806

Jason Kidd

Point Guard, Dallas Mavericks

■ ■ ■ ■ ■ ■ ■ ■ ■ ■ ■ ■ ■ ■ ■ ■

As a freshman at the University of California, Berkeley, Jason led his team to victory over Duke in the second round of the NCAA Tournament. After staying in school for two brilliant seasons, Kidd came to the NBA in 1994 with high expectations. In his first season with the Mavericks, Kidd played so impressively that he was named Co-Rookie of the Year. Kidd's greatness continued into his second season when he was named as a starter in the 1996 NBA all-star game.

> **So You Want to Know—**
> If Kidd had any competition at the University of California? If anyone, it was probably Jason's roommate. Jason's college teammate and roommate was Los Angeles Clippers star Lamond Murray.

Birthday Beat
March 23, 1973

Cool Credits
➤ Led St. Joseph's of Alameda to the California State High School Championship, 1991, 1992
➤ High School Player of the Year, California, 1991, 1992

➤ Freshman of the Year at the University of California, 1993
➤ Selected 2nd overall in the 1994 Draft
➤ Named to the all-rookie team, 1994
➤ NBA all-star, 1996

Vital Stats

➤ Height: 6'4"
➤ Weight: 210
➤ Birthplace: San Francisco, California
➤ Current residence: Oakland, California
➤ Favorite food: Chinese
➤ Hobby: playing baseball
➤ Nickname: The Whiz Kid

Jason Kidd
c/o Dallas Mavericks
777 Sports St.
Dallas, TX 75207

Alexi Lalas

Defenseman, New England Revolution

□ □ □ □ □ □ □ □ □ □ □ □ □ □ □ □ □ □ □

*L*alas is unquestionably the most popular American soccer player ever. In 1994, Lalas became a household name as he led the United States into the second round of the World Cup for the first time in over fifty years. Now, as member of the New England Revolution, Lalas is attempting to lift U.S. soccer to the status it holds in Europe and South America. While Lalas is best known for his long hair, goatee, and flashy style, he is also regarded as one of the best soccer players in the world.

Cool Credits

➤ All-American at Rutgers University, 1991
➤ Only American to be named to the 1994 World Cup all-star team
➤ First American ever to play in Italy's top league, the A League
➤ One of the first Americans to agree to play in the new U.S. Major League Soccer Federation

---

So You Want to Know—

What kind of music Alexi plays? Lalas isn't much of a fan of today's grunge music. He prefers classic 70s rock like the Rolling Stones, Bob Dylan, and Led Zeppelin.

Birthday Beat
June 1, 1970

Vital Stats

➤ Height: 6'3"
➤ Weight: 195
➤ Birthplace: Detroit, Michigan
➤ Current residence: Boston, Massachusetts
➤ Family ties: Younger brother Greg also plays in the Major League Soccer Federation, for the Tampa Bay Mutiny.
➤ Favorite food: pasta
➤ Hobby: playing the guitar
➤ Musical feats: Alexi has two CDs out and played backup guitar on the Kiss tribute record.

➤ T.V. appearances: *The Late Show with David Letterman* and *The Tonight Show with Jay Leno*

Alexi Lalas
c/o U.S. Soccer Federation
1801-11 South Prairie Ave.
Chicago, IL 60616

Greg Maddux
Pitcher, Atlanta Braves

▼▼▼▼▼▼▼▼▼▼▼▼▼▼▼▼▼▼▼

Maddux has proven over the past four years why he is widely regarded as one of the best pitchers ever to play the game. He is the only pitcher to win the Cy Young Award for best pitcher in the league four times, and is only the second pitcher in history to win the award with two different teams (Cubs and Braves). Maddux hurled the Braves to two World Series and played a major role in 1995's win over the Indians to give the Braves their first championship since 1957.

Birthday Beat
April 14, 1966

52

Cool Credits

➤ Cy Young Award Winner, 1992–1995
➤ Led National League in ERA, 1993–1995
➤ Golden Glove Award, 1990–1995
➤ Named to National League all-star team, 1989–1995

Vital Stats

➤ Height: 6'0"
➤ Weight: 175
➤ Birthplace: San Angelo, Texas
➤ Current residence: Las Vegas, Nevada

So You Want to Know—

How Maddux gives back to the Atlanta community? Greg and his wife Kathy head the Maddux Foundation, which gives Braves tickets to underprivileged children.

Greg Maddux
c/o The Atlanta Braves
P.O. Box 4064
Atlanta, GA 30302

Mark Messier

Center, New York Rangers

■ ■ ■ ■ ■ ■ ■ ■ ■ ■ ■ ■ ■ ■ ■ ■ ■

Whether it was on the Edmonton Oilers or on the New York Rangers, Messier has been a key part of six Stanley Cup wins. After he led the Rangers to the Cup in 1994, Messier became the first player to ever be the captain of two different Stanley Cup winning teams. Messier is a leader on the ice and in the clubhouse, both by his positive attitude and by setting a good example for others to follow. Messier is a perennial All-Star and reigns as one of the best hockey players of all time.

So You Want to Know—

How close Wayne Gretzky and Messier have been over the years? Messier replaced Gretzky on the Indianapolis Racers in the junior hockey leagues before they became teammates on the Oilers. Both men remain close friends to this day.

Birthday Beat

January 18, 1961

Vital Stats

➤ Height: 6'1"
➤ Weight: 205
➤ Birthplace: Edmonton, Alberta
➤ Current residence: Edmonton, Alberta
➤ Favorite food: bratwurst
➤ T.V. appearances: *The Howard Stern Show* and *The Late Show with David Letterman*

Cool Credits

➤ Made his NHL debut at the age of eighteen with the Oilers, 1979
➤ Won Stanley Cup with Edmonton Oilers, 1984, 1985, 1987, 1988, 1990
➤ Won Stanley Cup with New York Rangers, 1994
➤ NHL all-star, 1983–1996

Mark Messier
c/o The New York Rangers
Madison Square Garden
4 Penn Plaza
New York, NY 10001

Dominique Moceanu

Olympic Gymnast

□ □ □ □ □ □ □ □ □ □ □ □ □ □ □ □

*A*t the age of only fourteen, Dominique's already the best gymnast in the United States and one of the best in the world. Dominique has been in gymnastics competitions since the age of four. While the United States is not generally known as one of the best places in the world for gymnastics, Moceanu is doing what she can to change all that. In 1995, she was the only American to win a medal at the World Championships when she brought home a silver and a bronze—not bad for a freshman in high school!

Cool Credits

➤ Junior National Champion, 1994
➤ Youngest Senior National Champion in U.S. history, 1995
➤ Won silver and gold medals at the World Championships, 1995

Birthday Beat

September 30, 1981

Vital Stats

➤ Height: 4'5"
➤ Weight: 70
➤ Birthplace: Hollywood, California
➤ Current residence: Houston, Texas
➤ Hobbies: reading, swimming, listening to country music
➤ Favorite events: balance beam and the floor exercise
➤ Favorite sports team: Houston Rockets

□ □ □ □ □ □ □ □ □ □ □ □ □ □ □ □ □ □

So You Want to Know—

What Dominique's parents gave up so their
daughter could become a champion?

Dominique's parents
Camelia and Dimitry,
both gymnasts in
Romania, took their
three-year-old
daughter to the
famous gymnastics
coach Bela Karolyi,
who has coached
such Olympic
champions as Mary
Lou Retton and
Nadia Comaneci.
Karolyi agreed to
coach Dominique
once she got a
little older. At the age of nine,
Dominique moved to Houston with her
parents and joined Karolyi's stable of champions.

Dominique Moceanu
c/o Karolyi's Gymnastics
17203 Bamwood Rd.
Houston, TX 77090

Cam Neely

Forward, Boston Bruins

▼▼▼▼▼▼▼▼▼▼▼▼▼▼▼▼▼▼▼▼▼

Birthday Beat
June 6, 1965

So You Want to Know—

How Neely got his big break into TV? Neely
holds the distinction of being the favorite player
of actor Dennis Leary, who was in such films as
The Sandlot and *Operation Dumbo Drop*. When
Leary was a spokesman for Nike, he let it be
known how much he would love to do a
commercial with Neely. The result? Nike's The
Cam Neely Workout commercial, in which both
Neely and Leary appear.

*C*am Neely's scoring and leadership are major reasons the Bruins have made the playoffs for more consecutive seasons than anyone in NHL history. Neely has been in the NHL for fourteen years and is a rare gem who seems to shine brighter and brighter the longer he plays. He maintains a rigorous off-season workout schedule in order to keep in the prime shape required to play professional sports. At thirty-one years old, Neely gives every indication that the best is yet to come.

Vital Stats

➤ Height: 6'1"
➤ Weight: 220
➤ Birthplace: Comox, British Columbia
➤ Current residence: Boston, Massachusetts
➤ Favorite food: Italian

Cool Credits

➤ Had a hat trick (three goals) against Oshawa in the Junior League Championships, 1983
➤ Drafted by the Vancouver Canucks in the first round of the 1983 NHL Draft
➤ Led NHL in power play goals, 1995

Cam Neely
c/o The Boston Bruins
One Fleet Center Way
Boston, MA 02030

Hideo Nomo
Pitcher, Los Angeles Dodgers

■ ■ ■ ■ ■ ■ ■ ■ ■ ■ ■ ■ ■ ■ ■

Being a national superstar in one country wasn't enough for Nomo. After an illustrious baseball career in Japan, he was convinced by Dodger manager Tommy Lasorda to test himself against the best players in the world. Nomo was a huge success in his first season in the majors. He started the all-star game and was chosen as the National League's Rookie of the Year.

Birthday Beat
August 31, 1968

So You Want to Know—

How many outstanding rookies the Dodgers have had? Recently, four. Hideo is the fourth consecutive Dodger to become Rookie of the Year. Mike Piazza, Eric Karros, and Raul Mondesi held that honor in '92, '93, and '94.

Vital Stats

➤ Height: 6'2"
➤ Weight: 210
➤ Birthplace: Osaka, Japan
➤ Current residence: Osaka, Japan and Los Angeles, California
➤ Nickname: Tornado

Cool Credits

➤ Led the majors in shutouts, strikeouts (236), and finished with the second best ERA in the country, 1995
➤ National League all-star, 1995
➤ Rookie of the Year, 1995
➤ National League Player of the Month, June 1995
➤ All-star all five years with the Kintetsu Buffaloes in Japan
➤ Won the Sawamura Award (Japanese equivalent of the Cy Young Award), 1990
➤ Won Olympic silver medal for Japan, 1988

Hideo Nomo
c/o The Los Angeles Dodgers
1000 Elysian Park Ave.
Los Angeles, CA 90012

Shaquille O'Neal

Center, Orlando Magic

□ □ □ □ □ □ □ □ □ □ □ □ □ □ □ □ □

Just five short years after its inception in 1990, the Orlando Magic made it to the NBA Finals. There is but one reason that the Magic rose to the NBA elite so quickly, and that reason is Shaquille O'Neal. O'Neal is one of the best centers in the game, and his aggressive backboard-breaking dunks have made him one of the most feared players in the NBA. But while opponents fear the 7'1" center, he has been embraced by kids throughout the world because of his cheery demeanor. O'Neal not only wants to be the best basketball player he can be, but he also wants to be as good a role model for children as his stepfather was for him.

So You Want to Know—

How Shaquille met Anfernee Hardaway? Shaquille met his current teammate Hardaway while filming the movie *Blue Chips* in 1993. The two played plenty of basketball together while working on the movie, and Shaq strongly suggested the Magic draft Hardaway. The result? The Magic took O'Neal's advice and ended up with possibly the best offensive pair in professional basketball.

Cool Credits

➤ All-American at Louisiana State University, 1991, 1992
➤ First pick in the NBA draft, 1992
➤ Rookie of the Year, 1993
➤ NBA scoring leader, 1995
➤ NBA all-star every season he has been in the league, 1993–1996

Vital Stats

➤ Height: 7'1"
➤ Weight: 305
➤ Birthplace: Newark, New Jersey
➤ Current residence: Islesworth, Florida
➤ Nicknames: Shaq, Shaq-Fu
➤ Favorite music: rap
➤ Favorite band: Fu-Schnickens, rap group

➤ Hobbies: acting, making rap albums.
➤ Musical feats: O'Neal has two albums out, and performed with the Fu-Schnickens on the *Arsenio Hall Show* in 1993.

Birthday Beat

March 6, 1972

Shaquille O'Neal
c/o Orlando Magic
Orlando Arena
One Magic Place
Orlando, FL 32801

Manny Ramirez

Outfielder, Cleveland Indians

▼▼▼▼▼▼▼▼▼▼▼▼▼▼▼▼▼▼▼▼▼▼▼

One of the main reasons the Cleveland Indians have become one of the best teams in the major leagues is Manny Ramirez. While Cleveland has long been packed with superstars like Jack McDowell, Albert Belle, and Orel Hershiser, the tribe needed another star to emerge to make them unbeatable. Ramirez filled the bill in 1995 when he batted .308 with 31 home runs and 107 RBIs. Ramirez was selected as an American League all-star team member in just his second season in the majors.

So You Want to Know—

How often balls fly out of Jacobs Field? Pretty often when Ramirez and teammate Albert Belle are hitting. In 1995 the two men combined for eighty-two home runs, the most hit by teammates in Cleveland Indian history. Not only that, the record was set in a season eighteen games shorter than usual.

Birthday Beat

May 30, 1972

Vital Stats

➤ Height: 6'0"
➤ Weight: 190
➤ Birthplace: Santo Domingo, Dominican Republic
➤ Current residence: Washington Heights, New York
➤ Favorite food: Mexican

Cool Credits

➤ Rookie of the Year Runner-up, 1994
➤ The *Sporting News* all-star team, 1995
➤ American League all-star, 1995

➤ Silver Slugger winner, 1995
➤ American League Player of the Month, May 1995

Manny Ramirez
c/o The Cleveland Indians
2401 Ontario St.
Cleveland, OH 44115

Jerry Rice

Wide Receiver, San Francisco 49ers

■ ■ ■ ■ ■ ■ ■ ■ ■ ■ ■ ■ ■

I t is impossible to open the NFL record book without seeing Rice's name over and over again. During his twelve years with the 49ers, Rice has literally rewritten the record book, as he holds virtually every receiving record there is. Rice is a player who seems to gain more receiving yards with every season he plays, which is a scary thought for NFL corner- backs who have to cover him. A definite Hall- of-Famer, Jerry Rice is the greatest receiver ever to play in the NFL.

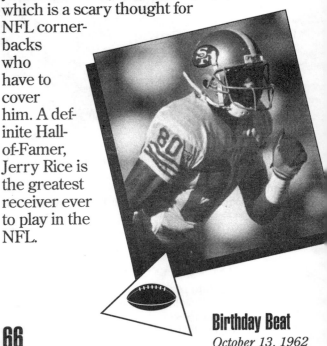

Birthday Beat
October 13, 1962

Cool Credits

➤ The *Sporting News* all-American at Mississippi Valley State, 1984
➤ First-round NFL draft choice by the 49ers, 1985
➤ Selected to the Pro Bowl, 1986–1996
➤ NFL MVP, 1989
➤ Super Bowl victories with 49ers, 1989, 1990, 1995
➤ Super Bowl MVP, 1989
➤ NFL record for most receiving yards in a season, 1995
➤ NFL record for most touchdowns in a career

Vital Stats

➤ Height: 6'2"
➤ Weight: 190
➤ Birthplace: Starkville, Mississippi
➤ Current residence: San Francisco, California
➤ Favorite food: Cajun

So You Want to Know—

What the other NFL teams were thinking? Very few NFL scouts knew much about Rice when he came out of Mississippi Valley State in 1984. The 49ers, however, had done their homework and traded up to the seventeenth pick in the first round to select Rice. The rest is history, as Rice has become one of the best players ever to play in the NFL.

Jerry Rice
c/o 49ers Football Club
4949 Centennial Blvd.
Santa Clara, CA 95054

Mitch Richmond

Shooting Guard, Sacramento Kings

❑ ❑ ❑ ❑ ❑ ❑ ❑ ❑ ❑ ❑ ❑ ❑ ❑ ❑ ❑ ❑ ❑ ❑

R ichmond has been a team leader since his college days at Kansas State, where he led the Wildcats to the Final Four in 1988. In the NBA, Richmond is a five time all-star and team captain of the Kings. Basketball experts believe Richmond is the second best shooting guard in the NBA, behind only Michael Jordan. Jordan himself is a big Richmond fan, and suggested to the United States Olympic Committee that Richmond be added to the Olympic Team. The USOC agreed, and added Richmond in April of 1996. Richmond first played on the Olympic basketball team in 1988, but did not play in 1992.

So You Want to Know—

If Richmond has team spirit? You bet he does. Richmond ordered a custom Porsche in purple and black so it would match the Kings' team colors.

□ □ □ □ □ □ □ □ □ □ □ □ □ □ □ □ □ □

Cool Credits

➤ 1st team all-American with Kansas State, 1988
➤ Olympic bronze medal, 1988
➤ NBA Rookie of the Year, 1989
➤ NBA all-star, 1992–1996
➤ 2nd Team all-NBA, 1993–95
➤ NBA all-star MVP, 1995
➤ Member of 1996 U.S. Olympic Basketball Team
➤ Led Sacramento to their first playoff appearance in ten years, 1996

Vital Stats

➤ Height: 6'5"
➤ Weight: 215
➤ Birthplace: Ft. Lauderdale, Florida
➤ Current residence: Sacramento, California
➤ Favorite food: barbecue chicken
➤ Nickname: Rock
➤ Hobbies: Nintendo, playing baseball

Birthday Beat
June 30, 1965

Mitch Richmond
c/o Sacramento Kings
One Sports Parkway
Sacramento, CA 95834

Cal Ripken, Jr.

Shortstop, Baltimore Orioles

Cool Credits

➤ American League Rookie of the Year, 1982
➤ American League all-star, 1983–1995
➤ American League MVP, 1983, 1991
➤ ESPN Athlete of the Year, 1996
➤ Most home runs ever hit by a shortstop (327)
➤ Golden Glove winner, 1991, 1995

Vital Stats

➤ Height: 6'4"
➤ Weight: 220
➤ Birthplace: Havre de Grace, Maryland
➤ Current residence: Reistertown, Maryland
➤ Favorite food: seafood
➤ Fun extravagance: Cal had a mini-amusement park built in his home for his children.

Birthday Beat

August 24, 1960

▼▼▼▼▼▼▼▼▼▼▼▼▼▼▼▼▼▼

On September 26, 1995, Ripken broke the record that no one ever thought would be broken—Lou Gehrig's record of playing in 2,130 consecutive games. While the streak is the primary thing Ripken will be remembered for, it is definitely not the only thing. Ripken is one of the best hitting shortstops ever to play the game. Ripken exemplifies everything that is good about sports in America with his hard work ethic,

> **So You Want to Know**—
> If Cal is worried about missing a game? Only in his dreams. Cal has a recurring nightmare in which he wakes up late and misses a game, breaking his record streak of consecutive games.

desire to win, refusal to give up, and his support of his teammates. He is a player both kids and adults can look to as a role model.

• •

Cal Ripken, Jr.
c/o The Tufton Group
333 Camden St.
Baltimore, MD 21201

• •

Rashaan Salaam

Running Back, Chicago Bears

■ ■ ■ ■ ■ ■ ■ ■ ■ ■ ■ ■ ■ ■

*R*ashaan Salaam won the 1994 Heisman Trophy while playing for the University of Colorado, Boulder. So when he joined the Bears organization, Chicago fans expected Salaam to be the savior of their running game, which suffered since Walter Payton's retirement. Salaam did not disappoint. As a rookie—and the NFL's youngest player —he ran for over 1,000 yards.

Cool Credits

➤ Fiesta Bowl MVP, 1994

➤ Heisman Trophy winner, 1994

➤ All-American, 1994

➤ Only the fourth player in NCAA history to rush for over 2,000 yards in a single season

➤ Led the NCAA with 24 touchdowns, 1994

> First round pick by the Bears in the 1995 NFL Draft

> NFC Offensive Rookie of the Year, 1995

So You Want to Know—

What Rashaan did with his Heisman trophy after he won it? On the plane back to Colorado from New York, Rashaan set the trophy next to him on the floor. When the plane hit some turbulence, the trophy rolled down the aisle and was dented. Once the trophy was fixed, Rashaan gave it to his mother.

Vital Stats

> Height: 6'1"
> Weight: 255
> Birthplace: San Diego, California
> Current residence: La Jolla, California
> Favorite food: Mexican
> Family ties: Rashaan's father, Sultan Salaam, played for the Cincinnati Bengals.
> Meaning of the name: Rashaan's full name means "righteous, faith, peace."

Birthday Beat

October 8, 1974

Rashaan Salaam
c/o The Chicago Bears
Soldier Field
Chicago, IL 60616

Pete Sampras

Tennis Player

□ □ □ □ □ □ □ □ □ □ □ □ □ □ □ □ □ □ □

There has never been a quieter or classier champion than Pete Sampras. While Sampras lacks the flash of Andre Agassi, the mouth of John McEnroe, or the flamboyance of Jimmy Connors, he possesses the talent of all three. Sampras is that rare player who is equally effective on all three tennis surfaces—clay, grass, and hardcourt. Perhaps that's one reason he's been rated the best tennis player in the world for three consecutive years.

Cool Credits

➤ Turned pro at the age of seventeen, 1988
➤ Became the youngest U.S. Open winner in history, 1990
➤ Won U.S. Open, 1993
➤ Won Wimbledon, 1993–1995
➤ Won Australian Open, 1994
➤ The fourth player in history to end three consecutive seasons as the No. 1 player in the world. (Jimmy Connors, John McEnroe, and Ivan Lendl are the others.)

Vital Stats

➤ Height: 6'1"
➤ Weight: 170
➤ Birthplace: Washington, D.C.
➤ Current residence: Tampa, Florida
➤ Hobby: playing Nintendo

➤ Favorite teams: Los Angeles Lakers and Dallas Cowboys

Birthday Beat

August 12, 1971

So You Want to Know—

What makes Sampras nervous? Is it playing Andre Agassi in a Grand Slam final? Is it meeting Queen Elizabeth II after winning Wimbledon? Was it his first match as a pro? None of the above. Sampras says the most nervous he's ever been was when he met Johnny Carson on *The Tonight Show* after winning the U.S. Open in 1990.

The Pete Sampras Fan Club
One Bowerman Dr.
Beaverton, OR 97005
or
Pete Sampras
c/o International Management Group
22 East 71st St.
New York, NY 10021

Deion Sanders

Defensive Back, Dallas Cowboys

▼▼▼▼▼▼▼▼▼▼▼▼▼▼▼▼▼▼▼

Before the 1994 season, Deion turned down lucrative offers from the New Orleans Saints and the Philadelphia Eagles to sign with the 49ers for about twenty-five percent of his market value in order to have a better chance at winning the Super Bowl. The result? The 49ers won the Super Bowl. For the 1995 season, Deion decided it was time to take his talent elsewhere, and he signed with the Dallas Cowboys. The result? The Cowboys won the Super Bowl. Is it just a coincidence, or is Deion one of the best defensive players ever to play in the NFL?

So You Want to Know—

If Deion is a good guy? Just because he's flashy doesn't mean he's not a role model. Deion has never touched alcohol or drugs in his entire life. He even fines himself $20 every time he cusses and then donates that money to charity.

Birthday Beat
August 9, 1967

Cool Credits

➤ All-American at Florida State, 1986–1988
➤ Led the Atlanta Braves to the World Series, 1992
➤ Played in NFL Pro Bowl, 1992–1994
➤ Super Bowl victories, 1994, 1995
➤ NFL Defensive Player of the Year, 1994
➤ Named to NCAA All-Century team for outstanding college players of the last 100 years for his play as cornerback at Florida State, 1996

Vital Stats

➤ Height: 6'1"
➤ Weight: 195
➤ Birthplace: Fort Meyers, Florida
➤ Current residence: Alpharetta, Georgia
➤ Nicknames: Neon Deion and Prime Time
➤ Favorite food: lobster
➤ Super scoring: Deion once scored a touchdown and hit a home run in the same week!
➤ Played for: New York Yankees, Atlanta Braves, Cincinnati Reds, San Francisco Giants
➤ Favorite cartoon characters: Road runner and Wile E. Coyote

Deion Sanders
c/o The Dallas Cowboys
One Cowboys Parkway
Irving, TX 75063

Emmitt Smith

Running Back, Dallas Cowboys

■ ■ ■ ■ ■ ■ ■ ■ ■ ■ ■ ■ ■ ■ ■ ■

Cool Credits

➤ All-American at the University of Florida, 1989, 1990
➤ First round pick by the Dallas Cowboys in the 1991 NFL Draft
➤ NFL MVP, 1993
➤ Led the Cowboys to Super Bowl victories, 1993, 1994, 1996
➤ Super Bowl MVP, 1993
➤ All-pro, 1991–1995

Vital Stats

➤ Height: 5'9"
➤ Weight: 210
➤ Birthplace: Escambia, Florida
➤ Current residence: Pensacola, Florida
➤ Favorite food: lasagna
➤ College: University of Florida, 1995
➤ Majored in: recreation

Birthday Beat
May 15, 1969

*N*FL teams heard that Smith was too small and too slow to play in the NFL when he came out of the University of Florida in 1991. The Dallas Cowboys knew better and decided to pick the two time all-American anyway. It seems to have been the right decision. At the time of the draft, Dallas was the worst team in the NFL. Today, just five years later, they have won three Super Bowls with Emmitt and have the most feared running game in the NFL. Emmitt finds the end zone the way a dog finds a steak, and he finds it often. In 1995, Smith broke John Riggins' record of most touchdowns in a season with twenty-four.

So You Want to Know—

Does Emmitt care about his fans? Emmitt is a regular contributor to the Make a Wish Foundation and donates a great deal of his time and money to bringing joy to handicapped and underprivileged children.

Emmitt Smith
c/o Emmitt Inc.
3300 N. Pace Blvd. #210
Pensacola, FL 32505

Sammy Sosa

Outfielder, Chicago Cubs

□ □ □ □ □ □ □ □ □ □ □ □ □ □ □ □ □ □ □ □

While many superstars in the major leagues possess either power or speed, Sosa is one of the precious few who has both. Sosa became the first player in Cubs history to steal thirty bases and hit thirty home runs in the same season— and did it twice! Named to the all-star team in 1995, he has already established himself as one of the top hitters in the major leagues.

Birthday Beat
November 12, 1968

Cool Credits

➤ Silver Slugger Award, 1995
➤ A member of the 30/30 club, for hitting 30 home runs while stealing 30 bases, 1993, 1995
➤ National League all-star, 1995
➤ Finished second in the league in home runs and RBIs, 1995

Vital Stats

➤ Height: 6'0"
➤ Weight: 190
➤ Birthplace: San Pedro de Macoris, Dominican Republic
➤ Current residence: Chicago, Illinois
➤ Favorite food: barbecued ribs

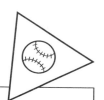

So You Want to Know—

How long Sosa has been playing professional baseball? Sosa was sixteen when he signed his first professional contract in the Dominican Republic. So, at just twenty-eight, he has already been a pro for twelve years.

Sammy Sosa
c/o The Chicago Cubs
Wrigley Field
1060 W. Addison Dr.
Chicago, IL 60611

Jerry Stackhouse

Shooting Guard, Philadelphia 76ers

▼▼▼▼▼▼▼▼▼▼▼▼▼▼▼▼▼▼▼▼

When Jerry Stackhouse was at the University of North Carolina, his playing was so strong that it evoked memories of former Tar Heel Michael Jordan. While Stackhouse insists he is not the second coming of Jordan, the comparison is inevitable. Both play shooting guard, both are 6' 6", and both were the third pick in the NBA draft. After just one season in the NBA, Stackhouse has proved worthy of the comparison by leading all rookies in scoring with a 19.2 points per game average.

So You Want to Know—

If Jerry graduated from college? Not yet. Even though Jerry left the University of North Carolina after his sophomore year, he promised his mother that he would go back to school and get his communication degree during the off-season. Stackhouse says it is a promise he intends to keep.

Birthday Beat
November 5, 1974

Cool Credits

➤ MVP of the McDonalds all-American High School Game, 1993
➤ *Sports Illustrated* College Player of the Year, 1995
➤ All-American at the University of North Caolina, 1995
➤ Led North Carolina to the Final Four, 1995
➤ NBA Rookie of the Month, March 1996
➤ All-rookie team, 1996

Vital Stats

➤ Height: 6'6"
➤ Weight: 220
➤ Birthplace: Kinston, North Carolina
➤ Current residence: Philadelphia, Pennsylvania
➤ Favorite food: chicken
➤ Nickname: Stack

Jerry Stackhouse
c/o Philadelphia Spectrum
3601 SouthBroad St.
Philadelphia, PA 19148

Kordell Stewart

Quarterback, Running Back, Wide Receiver, Pittsburgh Steelers

S tewart was a triple-threat for Pittsburgh in 1995. Kordell was originally drafted as a quarterback, but he showed his willingness to help his team by agreeing to play wide receiver and running back.

Kordell became so popular with fans in his rookie season that he was the Pittsburgh player selected to "Go to Disneyland" by Disney if the Steelers had beaten the Cowboys in Super Bowl XXX. While Stewart is fast becoming known for his versatility in the NFL, he will always be remembered for his sixty-four-yard Hail Mary touchdown pass in the final seconds to beat Michigan in 1994.

Cool Credits

➤ 2nd team all-American, 1994
➤ Won ESPN's ESPY Awards in 1995 for College Football Play of the Year, and in 1996 for NFL Play of the Year
➤ Led the University of Colorado to a No. 3 ranking, 1995
➤ MVP of Fiesta Bowl, 1995

Vital Stats

➤ Height: 6'1"
➤ Weight: 215
➤ Birthplace: New Orleans, Louisiana
➤ Current residence: Marrero, Louisiana
➤ Hobbies: cutting hair, playing Sega Genesis
➤ Fave Sega game: College Football 1995

Birthday Beat

October 16, 1972

So You Want to Know—

How many nicknames Stewart has? Two. The world has come to know him as "Slash" because of the slashes dividing the positions he plays: quarterback (slash) running back (slash) wide receiver. Stewart's friends just call him "Kordy."

Kordell Stewart
c/o Pittsburgh Steelers
Three Rivers Stadium
Pittsburgh, PA 15219

Damon Stoudamire

Point Guard, Toronto Raptors

☐ ☐ ☐ ☐ ☐ ☐ ☐ ☐ ☐ ☐ ☐ ☐ ☐ ☐ ☐ ☐

With their first draft pick, the brand-new Toronto Raptors chose Damon Stoudamire. The local fans booed. After hearing that Toronto fans were not happy with his selection, Stoudamire told reporters, "That's okay, because they don't know me yet. But once they get to know me, they'll love me."

He was right. Less than a year later, Stoudamire is a hero in Toronto. With his excellent playing and positive attitude, he

has been the bright spot in a relatively bleak season for the expansion team. Stoudamire is the player the Raptors will build around in hopes of becoming a future NBA force.

Birthday Beat
September 3, 1973

□ □ □ □ □ □ □ □ □ □ □ □ □ □ □ □ □ □

So You Want to Know—

Who helped Damon get drafted? A lot of teams didn't want to draft Damon when he came out of college, because of his size. This was the same thing people said about the man who drafted Stoudamire, Raptors President, Isiah Thomas.

"He reminds me of me," Thomas said after drafting Stoudamire. Not a bad thing to hear from a potential Hall-of-Famer.

Cool Credits

➤ All-American at the University of Arizona, 1994, 1995
➤ All-Pac10, 1993–1995
➤ Led Arizona to the Final Four in Goodwill Games, 1993
➤ NBA Rookie of the Month, November 1995
➤ NBA Rookie of the Year, 1996

Vital Stats

➤ Height: 5'10"
➤ Weight: 170
➤ Birthplace: Portland, Oregon
➤ Current residence: Toronto, Ontario

Damon Stoudamire
c/o Toronto Raptors
Waterpark Place
20 Bay Street Suite 1702
Toronto, Ont. MSJ2N8

Sheryl Swoopes
Guard, United States Olympic Basketball Team

Cool Credits
➤ All-American at Texas Tech University, 1992, 1993
➤ Southwest Conference Player of the Year, 1992, 1993
➤ Collegiate Player of the year, 1993
➤ Led the United States to the Gold Medal at the 1993 Goodwill Games
➤ Member of the 1996 Olympic Team

Birthday Beat
May 25, 1971

Vital Stats
➤ Height: 6'0"
➤ Weight: 145
➤ Birthplace: Brownfield, Texas
➤ Current residence: Houston, Texas
➤ Nickname: Swoop
➤ Family ties: learned to play basketball from her brothers, who double-teamed her on the court.

▼▼▼▼▼▼▼▼▼▼▼▼▼▼▼▼▼▼▼▼▼▼▼▼

*S*woopes has single-handedly lifted women's basketball to another level in the United States. After leading Texas Tech to the National Championship in 1993, Swoopes played professionally in Europe, because the U.S. did not have a women's professional league. Thanks in part to Swoopes, that is soon to change. The NBA is sponsoring a women's league to begin play in 1996. Swoopes is the "female Michael Jordan" and has proven that she is the best female basketball player in the world by winning championships at every level.

So You Want to Know—
If women can have basketball shoes named after them? Michael Jordan, Shaquille O'Neal, Grant Hill, Patrick Ewing, and Penny Hardaway all have shoes named after them. When Nike introduced "Air Swoopes" in 1995, Sheryl became the first woman to have that distinction.

• •

Sheryl Swoopes
c/o The United States Olympic Team
One Olympic Plaza
Colorado Springs, CO 80909

• •

Frank Thomas

First Baseman, Chicago White Sox

■ ■ ■ ■ ■ ■ ■ ■ ■ ■ ■ ■ ■ ■ ■

*O*ne cannot help but sit in awe after watching Frank Thomas hit a home run. And he does it quite often. He has become one of the premier power hitters in the game, evoking memories of Reggie Jackson and Dave Winfield with his massive power. Not just a power hitter, he hits for average as well. Thomas is also one of the best fielders in the American League.

Birthday Beat
May 27, 1968

■ ■ ■ ■ ■ ■ ■ ■ ■ ■ ■ ■ ■ ■ ■ ■ ■ ■

Vital Stats

➤ Height: 6'5"
➤ Weight: 260
➤ Birthplace: Columbus, Georgia
➤ Current residence: Chicago, Illinois
➤ Nickname: The Big Hurt
➤ Favorite food: southern fried chicken

Cool Credits

➤ All-American at University of Auburn, 1988–1989
➤ First pick in the 1989 draft
➤ American League all-star, 1993–1996
➤ American League MVP, 1993, 1994

So You Want to Know—

How Thomas is connected to football? Thomas played football at the University of Auburn with another famous player . . . Bo Jackson!

Frank Thomas
c/o The Chicago White Sox
Comiskey Park 333 W. 35th St.
Chicago, IL 60616

Jacque Villeneueve

Race Car Driver

□ □ □ □ □ □ □ □ □ □ □ □ □ □ □ □ □ □

*I*t is rare for any driver to have much of an impact on the racing circuit in his first two years. Jacque Villeneueve, however, has already had a racing career that most can only dream about. In 1994, Jacque's rookie season on the circuit, he finished an unbelievable second at the Indianapolis 500. With such a spectacular start, many were predicting a fall for the Canadian-born racer. Jacque proved them wrong when he won the Indianapolis 500 in 1995. At just twenty-five years old, it is a good bet that we will be hearing from Jacque for many years to come.

Cool Credits

➤ Rookie of the Year, 1994
➤ Finished second in the Indianapolis 500, 1994
➤ Won the Indianapolis 500, 1995
➤ Youngest driver in history to surpass $1,000,000 in winnings

Birthday Beat
April 9, 1971

□ □ □ □ □ □ □   □

Vital Stats

➤ Height: 5'10"
➤ Weight: 175
➤ Birthplace: St. Jean d'Iberville, Quebec
➤ Current residence: Indianapolis, Indiana
➤ Family ties: Jacque's father Gilles Villeneueve was a former Grand Prix driver, and one of the best ever from Canada.

➤ Languages: speaks both French and English fluently

So You Want to Know—

What gave Jacque his love for racing? When Jacque was growing up in Canada, his father was a famous racer. When eight-year-old Jacque's father died tragically during a race, Jacque resolved to become the best driver in the world in his father's honor. It's a good bet he's done his father proud.

• •

Jacque Villeneueve
c/o Indianapolis 500
500 Market St.
Indianapolis, IN 46203

• •

Steve Young

Quarterback, San Francisco 49ers

▼▼▼▼▼▼▼▼▼▼▼▼▼▼▼▼▼▼▼▼

*F*ew athletes would be able to fill Joe Montana's shoes. While Young can never make San Franciscans forget Montana, he has definitely made a name of his own after leading the 49ers to the Super Bowl Championship in 1995. Young has been an all-pro each season he has started for the 49ers, and has made his mark as one of the best quarterbacks in the NFL by throwing six touchdown passes in the 1988 Super Bowl. Young is a rare breed, a quarterback who is able to run and throw, giving him more versatility and making the 49ers offense even more dangerous.

94

So You Want to Know—

What Young will do after football? Young went back to school during the off-season and is the only player in the NFL who has his law degree. He plans to practice law once his professional football career is over.

Cool Credits

➤ All-American at BYU, 1983
➤ NFC all-pro team, 1992–1995
➤ NFL Player of the Year, 1993, 1994
➤ Super Bowl victories, 1990, 1995
➤ Super Bowl MVP, 1995
➤ Set Super Bowl Record with six touchdowns against San Diego, 1995

Birthday Beat

October 11, 1961

Vital Stats

➤ Height: 6'2"
➤ Weight: 200
➤ Birthplace: Salt Lake City, Utah
➤ Current residence: Palo Alto, California
➤ Nickname: Forever Young
➤ Favorite food: Italian
➤ College: Brigham Young University

Steve Young
c/o 49ers Football Club
4949 Centennial Blvd.
Santa Clara, CA. 95054

Photo Credits